Introduction

If you love sugar modelling and adore animals, Marzipan Magic is just for you. Each model is kept simple and marzipan is a wonderfully versatile medium to use, so you'll find you can achieve great results, even if you've never tried marzipan modelling before.

Try to put lots of character into your subject as this makes all the difference. Study the animal you are going to make before you start and soon you will develop your own unique style.

When dressing your animals you don't need many clothes to define their personality. Keep it simple (like the mortar board on Top Dog) and you can create some great characters.

Once you have mastered these easy techniques, you can design cakes on which to place your characters, an ideal way to make a celebration extra special. To get you started, you'll find four projects at the back of this book.

Have fun creating your own marzipan magic,

Maisie

For my grandsons, Joshua, George, Taylor and William

First published in March 2003 by b. Dutton Publishing Limited, Alfred House, Hones Business Park, Farnham, Surrey, GU9 8BB.

Reprinted in December 2004, June 2005, December 2006 and July 2007

Copyright: Maisie Parrish 2003

ISBN10: 0-9532588-6-6

ISBN13: 978-0-9532588-6-4

All rights reserved.

No part of this publication may be reproduced, stored in a retrieval system or transmitted in any form or by means electronic, mechanical, photocopying, recording, or otherwise, without prior written permission of the copyright owner. A catalogue record of this book is available from the British Library.

Maisie Parrish has asserted her right under the Copyright, Designs and Patents Act, 1988, to be identified as the author of this work.

Publisher: Beverley Dutton

Editor: Jenny Stewart

Design: Sarah Richardson

Photography: Alister Thorpe

Printed in Spain

My sincere thanks to the publishing team for their professional help and guidance in the making of this book

Contents

Working with Marzipan

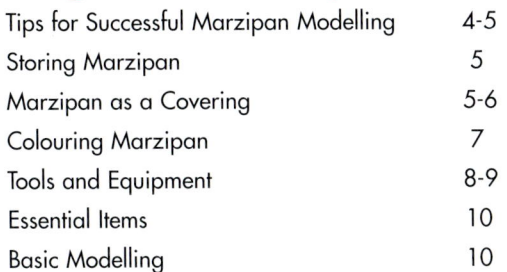

Tips for Successful Marzipan Modelling	4-5
Storing Marzipan	5
Marzipan as a Covering	5-6
Colouring Marzipan	7
Tools and Equipment	8-9
Essential Items	10
Basic Modelling	10

Modelling Animals

In the Field:	Knit One, Purl One	12-13
	Moo Cows	14-15
By the Pond:	Dancing Ducks	16-17
	Frolicking Frogs	18-19
Wildlife:	Baby Bunny	20-21
	Happy Hedgehogs	22-23
Canine Characters:	Top Dog	24-25
	Policeman Pooch	26-27
	Santa's Helpers	28-29
	Sheepdog Chef	30-31
	Bulldog Boss	32-33
Feline Friends:	Kissing Kitties	34-35
	Purrrfectly Matched	36-38

Projects

Spring:	Moo Cow Meadow	40-41
Summer:	Ducks on Swan Lake	42-43
Autumn:	Hibernating Happy Hedgehogs	44-45
Winter:	Sleigh Ride	46-47

Templates

48

Stockists

Inside Back Cover

Working with Marzipan

Marzipan is available in three main types, white (or neutral), yellow and raw sugar marzipan. White marzipan has the best texture and consistency for modelling as it takes colour well and is not too sticky. It is also ideal for covering cakes (see opposite). There are many brands of marzipan available, so when choosing which brand to use it is important that the marzipan has a smooth texture. Good-tasting marzipan will have an almond content of at least 23.5%, so do check this on the label. Nut-free coverings are also available for those with nut allergies. All the models and projects in this book were created using Squires Kitchen (SK) Marzipan, a smooth, ready-to-use paste which has a high almond content.

Although most people prefer to use commercial marzipan, you can, of course, make your own. Recipes for marzipan and nut-free paste can be found in cookery and cake decorating books.

For a great-tasting chocolate marzipan, blend equal amounts of marzipan and Squires Kitchen Dark or White Cocoform (modelling chocolate) together. Chocolate marzipan can be modelled and stored in the same way as marzipan.

Tips for Successful Marzipan Modelling

Marzipan should be kneaded gently before it can be modelled. This ensures it is soft and pliable, making it easy to work with.

Marzipan is best worked with at room temperature. Any marzipan you are not working with should be kept covered to prevent it from drying out. Plastic sandwich bags are ideal for this purpose. If the marzipan becomes too dry and cracks, knead a little white vegetable fat into it to make it more supple.

When rolling out marzipan, you can prevent it from sticking in one of a number of ways: roll out between two sheets of wax paper or plastic wrap; dust the work top with icing sugar; or grease the work surface with a little white vegetable fat. When you are moulding marzipan, you can use a little icing sugar or white vegetable fat on your hands to prevent the marzipan from sticking.

When marzipan is warm and pliable, it will stick to itself. However, if it has become a little dry, brush a small amount of Squires Kitchen (SK) Edible Glue onto the surface with a small brush and gently press the pieces together. Where you have two very hard parts to glue together, try mixing some marzipan and edible glue together with a palette knife to a tacky paste and apply. Leave to dry with support if necessary.

If extra support is required, for example when attaching the limbs, hands, feet and head to a model, insert a length of dry spaghetti into one of the pieces. Push the other piece onto the protruding spaghetti and add a little edible glue if required. Allow to dry. Remember that, although dry spaghetti is edible, it should be removed before the model is eaten.

For fine modelling and for pieces that need to support weight, such as legs for standing models, knead in 1 teaspoon of gum tragacanth per 250g of marzipan. This will make the marzipan firmer so it will hold its shape when dry.

Storing Marzipan

If stored correctly, marzipan has a long shelf life. Unopened packs of marzipan should be kept in cool, dry conditions away from sunlight.

Once opened, marzipan must be kept sealed to prevent it from drying out. Wrap tightly in several layers of plastic wrap and keep in a cool, dry place at room temperature.

For prolonged storage, marzipan that has been opened can be frozen. For best results, cut into small pieces and wrap tightly in several layers of plastic wrap before freezing. Allow the marzipan to defrost at room temperature, ensuring it has thoroughly thawed before use. Do not heat in a microwave as this may alter the consistency of the marzipan.

Marzipan as a Covering

While the main focus of this book is modelling with marzipan, it is a versatile medium which lends itself well to covering cakes and boards. These techniques are used in the four cake projects at the back of this book (pages 39-47).

Covering a cake drum

1. Prepare a non-stick board by rubbing a little white vegetable fat onto the surface. (If you find there is too much fat on the board, wipe off the excess with a piece of kitchen towel.) Knead the marzipan gently to make it supple, then roll out on the greased board. You can use a dusting of icing sugar instead of vegetable fat to stop the marzipan from sticking, but this can leave white marks on the marzipan.

2. Carefully lift the marzipan from the board and place over the cake drum. Roll over the marzipan lightly so that it sticks to the board, then trim off any excess paste from around the edge using a sharp marzipan knife.

3. Trim the board with 15mm wide ribbon to finish and secure with non-toxic stick glue or double-sided sticky tape.

Covering a cake

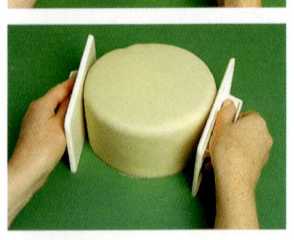

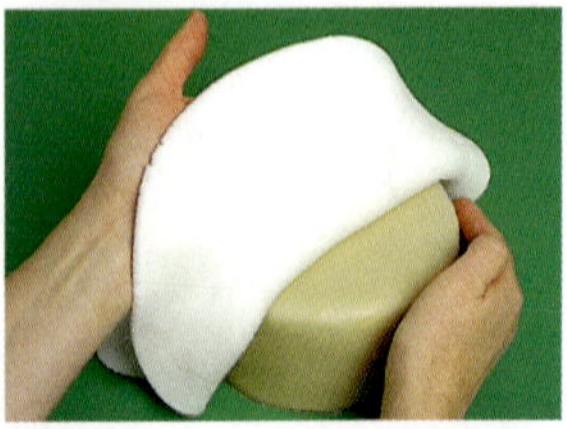

1. Brush the edge of the cake top with apricot glaze. Make a long sausage of marzipan and place around the edge so that the top of the cake has a level, flat surface. (Note that this step is not necessary for covering a spherical cake, as used in Moo Cow Meadow, pages 40-41.)

2. Fill in any holes on the surface of the cake with small pieces of marzipan to create a smooth surface for covering.

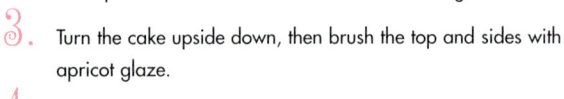

3. Turn the cake upside down, then brush the top and sides with apricot glaze.

4. Knead enough marzipan to cover the cake in one piece. Roll out on a greased non-stick board using the same method as for covering a cake drum, then lift the marzipan and place over the cake. Use the palm of your hand or a cake smoother to gently smooth over the surface of the cake. Carefully ease out any pleats and creases around the sides of the cake, then trim away the excess marzipan around the base of the cake using a sharp marzipan knife. For spherical cakes, bring the paste together at the base of the cake and smooth as much as possible.

5. Smooth the top and sides once more with cake smoothers. Place the covered cake onto the prepared cake drum.

If you wish to add a layer of sugarpaste to cover the marzipanned cake, brush the marzipan with a little clear spirit such as gin or vodka, then follow the instructions for covering a cake with marzipan.

Colouring Marzipan

Paste colours

To colour marzipan, knead in a little Squires Kitchen (SK) Paste Food Colour a little at a time using a cocktail stick. To disperse the colour easily, moisten your finger with a little cooled, boiled water and work the colour over the paste, then knead well. It is worth remembering that a little colour goes a long way and it is easier to make the colour more intense than to make it paler.

To colour marzipan white, you will need to use more colour than usual. If too much paste colour is used, it will alter the consistency of the marzipan, making it too soft to work with. The best way to overcome this problem is to use both Squires Kitchen (SK) Edelweiss Paste and Dust Food Colours. This method can be used for particularly strong and vibrant colours where a paste and dust is available in one colour.

Liquid colours

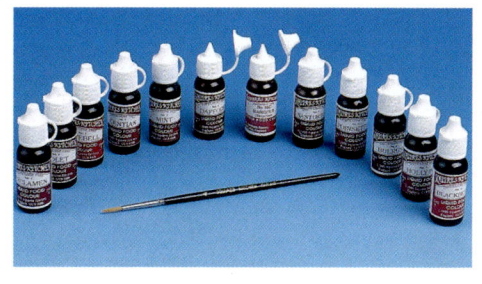

Squires Kitchen (SK) Liquid Food Colours are ideal for painting details onto the surface of marzipan models. For best results, leave the finished model for two hours so that the marzipan skins over. This will prevent the colour from bleeding. To dilute liquid colour, use a little clear alcohol (e.g. gin or vodka) as colour diluted with water is more likely to run and bleed. Use a fine artist's brush to apply the colour.

Dust colours

A broad spectrum of Squires Kitchen (SK) Dust Food Colours are available, including pastel and lustrous shades, and can be mixed together to create virtually any colour. Dust colours are used to add a subtle tint, e.g. for blushing cheeks, and lustre dust colours to add a sparkle. For best results, leave the finished marzipan model to dry for two hours before applying dust colour. Use a dry, fan-shaped paintbrush and apply a thin layer of colour at a time. Brush on more dust for a deeper shade.

Tools and Equipment

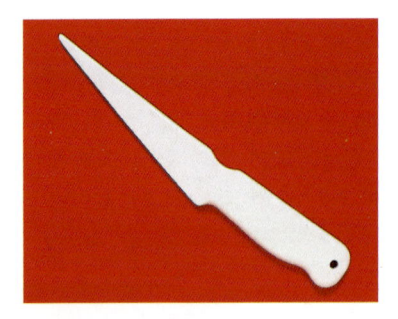

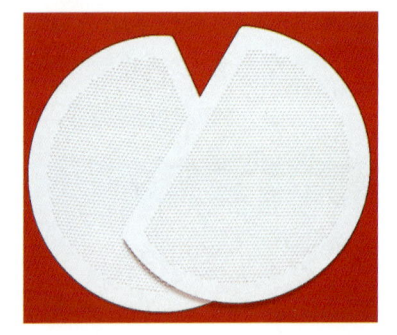

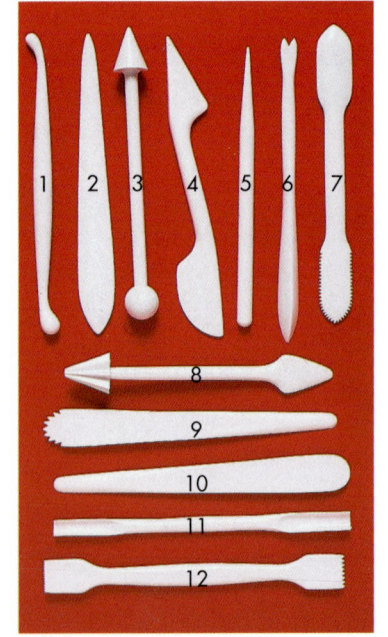

Squires Kitchen (SK) Marzipan Knife

A large, sharp plastic knife which glides through the marzipan. It has a smooth surface to prevent marzipan from sticking to it.

Squires Kitchen (SK) Texture Boards

Squires Kitchen Texture Boards are made of firm food-grade plastic, so you can roll the marzipan in-between the boards or push them onto rolled-out paste to achieve a pimple effect. They are ideal for creating an interesting texture on a covered cake (for example, Moo Cow Meadow, pages 40-41), for creating mesh or tulle effects and can be used to make pieces of marzipan fruit, golf balls and to texture clothing.

Squires Kitchen (SK) Marzipan Modelling Tools

A set of 12 modelling tools designed specifically for marzipan modelling. This means they are easy to handle, have a smooth surface to prevent the marzipan from sticking and are useful for many different purposes, as shown opposite.

Tool no.	Uses
1	Both ends can be used for making indentations such as eyes and mouth and can also be used to hollow out the inside of a shape or thin petals and leaves.
2	A tool useful for smoothing joins and marking veins on leaves.
3	The rounded end is useful for moulding a hollow shape from a ball of marzipan; the pointed end is useful for hollowing out cones and making fruit.
4	A cutting tool for making clean straight cuts and markings. There is no need to have a small knife as this does the job perfectly.
5	Both ends can be used for making eye sockets, nostrils and buttons; the pointed end can be used to frill paste.
6	The serrated end can be used for making rough textures for feathers, grass or wood; the rounded end creates a smooth indentation or channel in marzipan.
7	The serrated end can be used to make stitch marks on curved or flat shapes and to texture clothing; the smooth end is useful for blending joins and smoothing paste.
8	The pointed, star-shaped end can be used to indent the top of fruit, make buttons and create a decorative pattern; the flat end can create parallel straight lines using the point as a guide and is useful for trellis work.
9	Use this tool to indent a shell pattern onto a cake or board for a quick finish; use the narrow end to smooth over paste when using moulds.
10	A blunt tool used to hollow out rounded shapes, make arches, and for smoothing marzipan.
11	An invaluable tool for marking smiles, eyes and eyebrows on faces; also useful for fish scales.
12	A double-ended serrated tool used for making deep or fine stitch marks, useful when making teddy bears and clothing.

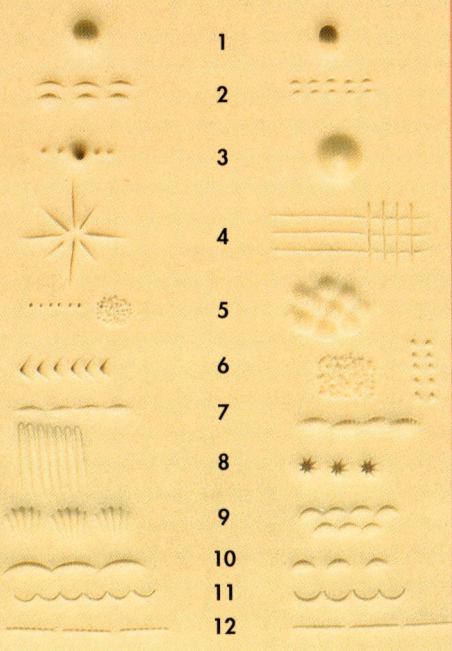

Duck's eyelids - using a no. 11 tool.

Cow's nostrils - using a no. 3 tool.

Dog's mouth - using a no. 11 and no. 5 tool.

Stitching on bunny - using a no. 7 tool.

Essential Items

When you start modelling with marzipan, it is worth making sure you have the following items to hand:

MATERIALS

Squires Kitchen (SK) Edible Glue
Dry spaghetti
White vegetable fat

EQUIPMENT

Non-stick polythene board
Non-stick polythene rolling pin
Pizza cutter/cutting wheel
SK Marzipan Knife
SK Marzipan Tool Set
SK Sugar Dough Press
Paintbrushes (various)

Keep all your tools and equipment clean and free from grease. All modelling tools, boards, cutters, etc. should be washed in warm soapy water and kept together (a pencil case is ideal). All edible materials should be stored according to the manufacturers' instructions.

Basic Modelling

Once you have mastered the simple techniques of creating basic forms, modelling any figure is straightforward. The basic shapes you will need are:

BALL

CONE

SAUSAGE

Modelling Animals

Knit One, Purl One

Materials

500g SK Marzipan

SK Dust Food Colours: Edelweiss, Soft Peach

SK Liquid Food Colours: Bulrush, Holly/Ivy

SK Paste Food Colours: Blackberry, Edelweiss, Fuchsia, Poinsettia

SK Edible Glue

Dry spaghetti

Equipment

Non-stick board and rolling pin

SK Marzipan Knife

SK Marzipan Tool Set

SK Sugar Dough Press

Paintbrushes

26 gauge florist wire: silver

Paper towel roll and small piece of card

Method

1. Cut 5cm off an empty paper towel roll to make a seat. Cut a circle out of card and glue over the top. Cover using 80g of marzipan and secure with edible glue. Stipple all over with Holly/Ivy Liquid Food Colour and leave to dry.

2. Make two knitting needles by rolling some Poinsettia coloured marzipan around two lengths of dry spaghetti. Colour a small piece of marzipan black and glue a knob on the end of each needle. Leave to dry.

3. Colour 400g of marzipan with Edelweiss Paste and Dust Food Colour. Take off a small piece and roll out fairly thinly. Cut out the jumper using the template (page 48) and texture with tool no. 12. Place a knitting needle on top and add a few strands of wool over the needle. Secure with edible glue.

4. To make the sheep, roll 30g of marzipan into a cone shape and place on top of the seat. Push a piece of dry spaghetti down through the body leaving 3cm showing at the top. Make two legs using 18g rolled into a sausage and cut diagonally in the centre. Mark a hoof at each rounded end with tool no. 4. Secure to the body and cross the legs over at the front. Fill a Sugar Dough press with white marzipan and squeeze out very short lengths 0.5cm long to make the wool. Chop off the strands using the no. 4 tool. Brush the body and legs with edible glue and cover with the wool. Make the arms in the same way, glue the empty needle into the right hand and secure to the body.

5. To make the head, roll 14g of marzipan into a cone shape. Mark the centre of the face with tool no. 4. Mark the nose in a 'V' shape and then the mouth with an inverted 'V', as shown. Push tool no. 5 into the mouth area and pull down slightly. Add two small ovals of black marzipan for the eyes. To make the ears, roll a small piece of white marzipan into a sausage shape, place a tiny roll of pink coloured marzipan inside and secure to the head. Make more wool to cover the head using the Sugar Dough press and make longer strands for the fringe. Roll 8g of white marzipan into a sausage shape, mark with tool no. 12 and secure to the back of the head.

6. Colour the front of the face using Soft Peach Dust Food Colour. Add a few eyelashes using a fine brush and Bulrush Liquid Food Colour. For the glasses, bend a short length of silver wire into a loop at each end, leaving a space in the middle for the bridge. Bend the bridge of the glasses and press onto the nose. Paint the hooves with Bulrush Liquid Food Colour.

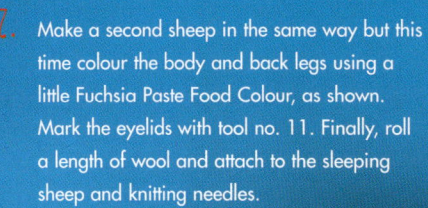

7. Make a second sheep in the same way but this time colour the body and back legs using a little Fuchsia Paste Food Colour, as shown. Mark the eyelids with tool no. 11. Finally, roll a length of wool and attach to the sleeping sheep and knitting needles.

A knitting sheep - who better to make a warm woolly jumper for the winter! You'll have great fun making the woolly coats for these sheep.

Moo Cows

Materials

60g SK Marzipan (for each cow)

SK Dust Food Colour: Edelweiss

SK Paste Food Colours: Blackberry, Edelweiss, Fuchsia, Sunflower, Teddy Bear Brown

SK Edible Glue

Equipment

Non-stick board and rolling pin

SK Marzipan Knife

SK Marzipan Tool Set

Cutters: calyx (small), circle (small)

Method

1. Colour approximately 35g of marzipan white using both Edelweiss Dust and Paste Food Colour. Take off 14g for the body and roll into a cone shape. Roll 10g into a sausage shape for the legs and cut into four. Make a diagonal cut at the top of each and attach to the body with edible glue. For the head, roll 6g of white marzipan into a cone shape and make a straight cut at the widest end, as shown. Roll two tiny cone shapes for the ears and secure to the side of the head.

2. For all the pink parts, colour 10g of marzipan with Fuchsia Paste Food Colour. Make an oval shape for the nose and mouth area. Use a no. 3 tool to make the nostrils, then make the mouth using the edge of a small circle cutter. Make the holes for the eyes using the pointed end of tool no. 5. Secure the head to the body. To make the udder, roll a small ball and place three smaller balls on the surface. Glue in-between the legs.

3. To make the hooves, roll a small teardrop shape from pink marzipan, make a cut at the pointed end, then fix to the leg. Mix 4g of marzipan with Blackberry Paste Food Colour to make the spots and tail. Roll two small balls and flatten in-between your fingers, then press these onto the body. Make the tail by rolling a thin strip of the

black marzipan, then mark the end with tool no. 4. Roll two small balls of black and glue inside the eye sockets. For a sleeping cow, use the smallest end of tool no. 11 to make the eyelids.

4. Colour 8g of marzipan with Sunflower Paste Food Colour to make the horns. Roll a tiny ball into a cone shape and secure one on either side of the head above the ears. Colour a small piece of marzipan with Teddy Bear Brown Paste Food Colour, roll out and cut out the hair using a small calyx cutter. Place in-between the horns.

These cows are really simple and great fun to make. You can make them on their own, but they look brilliant in a field together.

Instructions for Moo Cow Meadow can be found on pages 40-41.

Dancing Ducks

Materials

40g SK Marzipan (for each duck)

SK Dust Food Colours: Edelweiss, Pastel Pink, Rose

SK Liquid Food Colour: Blackberry

SK Paste Food Colours: Blackberry, Edelweiss, Nasturtium, Sunflower

SK Edible Glue

Dry spaghetti

Equipment

Non-stick board and rolling pin

SK Marzipan Knife

SK Marzipan Tool Set

Paintbrushes

Cutter: calyx (small)

Foam pieces (optional)

Method

1. To make a dancing duck, colour 30g of marzipan white using both Edelweiss Paste and Dust Food Colour. You will also need to colour approximately 4g of marzipan Nasturtium, 2g Sunflower and a tiny piece Blackberry for each duck.

2. To make the body, roll 12g of white marzipan into a cone shape, then pull out some paste at the back for the tail, as shown. Push a piece of dry spaghetti down through the body, leaving some showing at the neck to support the head.

3. Make the legs from 4g of Nasturtium marzipan divided in half. Roll each piece into a long, thin cone shape, flatten the end and cut out two 'V' shapes for the webbed feet. Carefully push a piece of dry spaghetti into each leg down to the ankle (if the leg is straight). Insert this into the base of the body.

4. Take 6g of white marzipan and divide in half for the wings. Make two cone shapes and flatten slightly, then mark the feathers using a no. 4 tool, as shown. Secure to the side of the body in the desired position with edible glue and support with foam if necessary until dry.

5. Roll 8g of white marzipan into a cone shape for the head. Slip the head over the spaghetti at the neck and use a little edible glue to secure it in place. For the beak, roll a small ball of Sunflower coloured marzipan and

flatten between your fingers. Make a straight cut across the middle and press onto the face. Mark the eyes with tool no. 5 and fill with tiny balls of black marzipan. Using the same tool, mark the nostrils on the top of the beak.

6. To make the feathers on the head, roll out some of the white marzipan and cut out a small calyx shape. Cut off two of the points and secure to the head. Paint eyelashes above the eyes using Blackberry Liquid Food Colour and a fine brush. Blush the cheeks with a mixture of Rose and Pastel Pink Dust Food Colours.

Instructions for Ducks on Swan Lake can be found on pages 42-43.

Because of their elegant wings and slender legs, ducks make great ballerinas! Each duck is made in the same way, then assembled to create an individual pose.

Frolicking Frogs

Materials

65g SK Marzipan (for each frog)

SK Dust Food Colour: Edelweiss

SK Liquid Food Colours: Holly/Ivy, Marigold

SK Paste Food Colours: Blackberry, Edelweiss, Leaf Green, Poinsettia

SK Silver Scintillo

SK Edible Glue

Equipment

Non-stick board and rolling pin

SK Marzipan Knife

SK Marzipan Tool Set

Paintbrushes

Cutter: circle (small)

Piping bag

Fine scissors

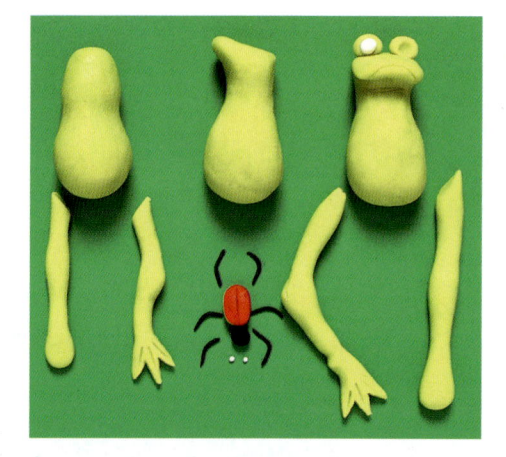

Method

1. Colour 60g of marzipan with Leaf Green Paste Food Colour to make each frog. The basic shape is the same for all the frogs shown here, just adapt a different position for the arms and legs.

2. Roll 35g of the green marzipan into a cone shape for the body, then roll between your fingers until it narrows at the neck area. Leave the top wide enough to shape the head.

3. To make the head, bring the top shape forward and flatten on the top. Mark the mouth with the edge of a circle cutter, then stand upright. Add two small balls at the top of the head and push tool no. 1 inside to make the eye sockets. Fill with two small balls of white marzipan coloured with Edelweiss Paste and Dust Food Colours.

4. For the back legs, divide 20g of the green marzipan in half and roll each piece into a sausage shape 9cm long. Reshape as shown and flatten the end. Using a no. 4 tool, cut out the feet and mark the top. Make a diagonal cut at the top of the leg using the same tool and secure to the body using edible glue. Position the legs as required.

5. The arms (or front legs) are made in exactly the same way as the back legs using 8g of marzipan. Secure to the front of the frog.

6. To make the ladybird, roll a small ball of Poinsettia coloured marzipan into an oval shape and mark the back down the centre with tool no. 4. Roll a small ball of black for the head and two tiny white balls for the eyes. To make the legs, roll a very thin sausage and cut into short lengths. Curve the legs with a paintbrush and attach to the body. Secure the ladybird to the tip of the frog's nose with a dot of edible glue.

7. To create a scaly effect, use a medium paintbrush and dab Holly/Ivy Liquid Food Colour randomly over the frog. Do the same with Marigold Liquid Food Colour. Paint a black pupil in each eye using a fine paintbrush, then outline with Marigold. Finally, outline the socket with black.

8. To create 'frog spawn', fill a piping back with some Silver Scintillo, snip off the tip of the bag and dot the Scintillo around the frog.

Frogs make an interesting addition to cakes when placed with fishing and water scenes. By altering their expressions, you can make the frogs humorous.

Baby Bunny

Materials

140g SK Marzipan

SK Dust Food Colour: Edelweiss

SK Paste Food Colours: Blackberry, Edelweiss, Fuchsia, Leaf Green, Nasturtium, Rose

SK Edible Glue

Dry spaghetti

Equipment

Non-stick board and rolling pin

SK Marzipan Knife

SK Marzipan Tool Set

Cutter: 5cm circle

White stamens

Method

1. Colour 125g of marzipan white using both Edelweiss Paste and Dust Food Colour. Take off approximately 105g and add a little Blackberry Paste Food Colour to make a very pale grey.

2. Roll 35g of the grey marzipan into a cone shape for the body. Stand this upright and lean it slightly backwards. Push a piece of dry spaghetti down through the neck and leave 3cm showing at the top.

3. Make a nappy using 10g of the white marzipan. Roll out and cut a 5cm circle. Next, cut off one third of the circle with the same cutter, as shown. Glue the largest piece onto the base of the body. Position the smaller piece vertically in the centre of the nappy. Texture the paste all over with the serrated edge on tool no. 7. Colour 4g of white marzipan with a little Fuchsia Paste Food Colour. Make a safety pin and glue to the front of the nappy.

4. To make the legs, divide 25g of grey marzipan in half and roll each piece into a sausage shape. Push up at one end to form the foot. Press onto the side of the body. Make stitch marks down the leg using tool no. 7. For the arms, divide 15g of grey marzipan in half, roll two sausage shapes and secure to the top of the body. Add stitch marks in the same way as for the legs.

5. Roll 20g of marzipan into a fat cone shape for the head and slip over the spaghetti. Make two small cone shapes for the cheeks and smooth onto the sides of the face with your finger. Add a round ball of white for the snout and a small pink nose. Roll two small white ovals for the eyes and add a black pupil to each. Make two tiny cigar shapes for the eyebrows and secure in place.

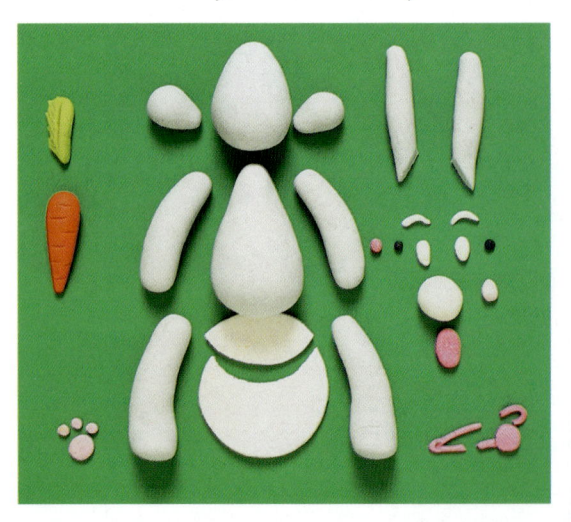

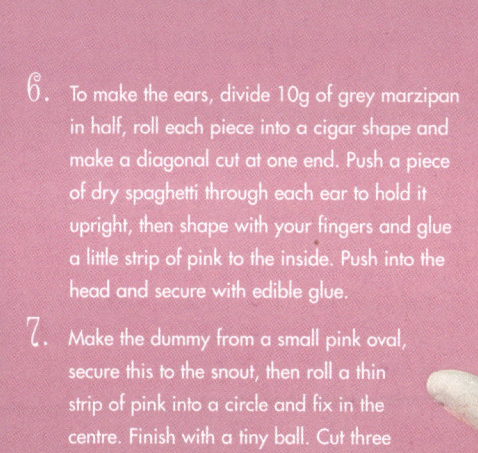

6. To make the ears, divide 10g of grey marzipan in half, roll each piece into a cigar shape and make a diagonal cut at one end. Push a piece of dry spaghetti through each ear to hold it upright, then shape with your fingers and glue a little strip of pink to the inside. Push into the head and secure with edible glue.

7. Make the dummy from a small pink oval, secure this to the snout, then roll a thin strip of pink into a circle and fix in the centre. Finish with a tiny ball. Cut three white flower stamens in half and push into the nose area.

8. Make a carrot from a tiny piece of marzipan coloured with Nasturtium Paste Food Colour. Roll into a cone and mark with tool no. 4. Colour a small piece of marzipan with Leaf Green Paste Food Colour and make three flattened cone shapes for leaves. Mark with tool no. 4 and push into the top of the carrot. Secure the carrot into the right hand of the rabbit with edible glue.

This chubby bunny is adorable in blue or pink and is a perfect decoration for a christening cake or baby's first birthday cake.

Happy Hedgehogs

Materials

90g SK Marzipan

SK Dust Food Colours: Bulrush, Chestnut, Rose, Soft Peach

SK Liquid Food Colour: Bulrush

SK Paste Food Colours: Blackberry, Daffodil

SK Edible Glue

Equipment

Non-stick board and rolling pin

SK Marzipan Knife

SK Marzipan Tool Set

Paintbrushes

Cutter: 2.5cm circle

Tweezers

Method

1. To make a large hedgehog, you will require approximately 90g of marzipan. Roll 45g of uncoloured marzipan into a fat cone shape for the body. Using a pair of tweezers, pinch all over the body to make it as spiky as possible.

2. Divide 8g of marzipan in half for the paws and roll each piece into a sausage shape. Flatten one end and mark the paws using a no. 4 tool. Secure to the body with edible glue.

3. For the head, roll 14g of marzipan into a cone shape. Pull out the nose and push upwards. Using a no. 4 tool, mark a line down the centre, as shown. Make the mouth by pressing a no. 11 tool either side of the centre line. Make a bottom lip by rolling a tiny amount of marzipan and placing this underneath. Roll two small balls for the cheeks and smooth them in.

4. Colour a small piece of marzipan with Daffodil Paste Food Colour. Roll two tiny balls for the eyes and place above and either side of the nose. Roll a small black ball for the nose.

5. To widen the head, roll a small sausage shape of marzipan and taper the ends.

Place this over the top of the head. Using a no. 4 tool, make upward strokes in the paste to form spikes. Add a little more marzipan at the back of the head and blend this in. Add tiny ears made from two cone shapes and blend in with tool no. 4. Leave to dry.

6. Dust all over the body with Chestnut Dust Food Colour. Using Bulrush Liquid Food Colour and a fine brush, paint the claws, outline the eyes and paint in the pupils.

7. Dust the face using Soft Peach Dust Colour, then mix in a little Rose Dust Colour to blush the cheeks. Dust the bottom lip and ears with the same colour.

Hedgehogs are very simple to make and they are a great subject for any celebration cake.

Instructions for Hibernating Happy Hedgehogs can be found on pages 44-45.

Top Dog

Materials

400g SK Marzipan

SK Dust Food Colour: Edelweiss

SK Paste Food Colours: Blackberry, Bluebell, Daffodil, Edelweiss, Poinsettia

SK Edible Glue

Dry spaghetti

Equipment

Non-stick board and rolling pin

SK Marzipan Knife

SK Marzipan Tool Set

Paintbrushes

Cutter: 2.5cm circle

Tweezers

Method

1. To make the books, colour 275g of marzipan white using both Edelweiss Paste and Dust Food Colour, 50g Poinsettia and 60g Bluebell. Weigh out 190g of white and make a block measuring 14cm x 12cm x 1.5cm. Cut in half to make two books. Using tool no. 4, mark lines all around the edges to resemble pages. Place the remaining white marzipan to one side as this will be used to make the 'Westie'.

2. Roll out the blue marzipan to make the book cover. Cut out a rectangle measuring 14cm x 8cm. Place the white pages on one edge and fold the cover up and over the top. Trim if necessary and secure in place with edible glue. Mark the spine of the book with the no. 4 tool. Make another book in the same way from the red marzipan.

3. Add some more Bluebell Paste Food Colour to the remaining blue marzipan. Roll out thinly and coat the surface with a thin layer of vegetable fat. Cut out the letters and secure to the books with edible glue.

4. To make the 'Westie', roll 35g of white marzipan into a cone shape. Push a piece of dry spaghetti down through the body leaving 3cm showing at the top. Using tool no. 4, mark the fur all over the body. Make two front legs by rolling 8g of white marzipan into a sausage shape, turn the rounded ends up for the feet and make a diagonal cut in the centre. Secure to the front of the dog and mark the fur, blending in the paste to hide the joins at the top of the legs. Mark the paws. Roll 8g of white marzipan into a cone shape for the back leg. Press onto the dog and mark the fur and paws. Add a tiny cone shape at the back for the tail, which should point upwards, and mark fur.

5. For the head, roll 18g of white marzipan into a cone shape and flatten at the front. Mark the centre with tool no. 4, then make the mouth with

tool no. 11. Pull the mouth down slightly with tool no. 5 and glue a small pink tongue inside. Mark the tongue with the same tool. Create eye sockets with the no. 5 tool and fill with small black balls (these can be left over from the mortarboard, below). Add a black nose. Make the fur for the face using a Sugar Dough press and glue in place. Add two pointed ears and paint pink inside using diluted Poinsettia Paste Food Colour.

6. Using a small piece of red marzipan, cut a thin strip for the collar and glue in place. Colour a tiny piece of marzipan yellow, make a disc and glue below the collar. Place the dog on top of the books.

7. To make the mortarboard, colour 10g of marzipan with Blackberry Paste Food Colour. Cut out a 2.5cm square and leave to dry. Roll a ball and pinch out a point at the back and front. Glue this on top of the dog's head, then add the top of the hat. To make the tassel, roll a small sausage shape, mark at one end with tool no. 4 and secure to the top of the hat.

8. To make the scroll, thinly roll out 10g of white marzipan. Cut a strip and roll up neatly, then add a black marzipan ribbon. Paint two black paw marks using a fine paintbrush and Blackberry Liquid Food Colour. Place on top of the books.

This West Highland white terrier (or 'Westie') is characterised by his short legs, coarse coat, stocky body and a short pointed tail.

Policeman Pooch

Materials

120g SK Marzipan

SK Dust Food Colour: Edelweiss

SK Liquid Food Colour: Blackberry

SK Paste Food Colours: Blackberry, Bluebell, Bulrush, Daffodil, Edelweiss, Poinsettia, Teddy Bear Brown

SK Edible Glue

Dry spaghetti

Equipment

Non-stick board and rolling pin

SK Marzipan Knife

SK Marzipan Tool Set

Paintbrushes

Cutters: circle (small), squares (small), star (small)

Method

1. Colour 70g of marzipan with Teddy Bear Brown Paste Food Colour. Divide the marzipan in half and roll one piece into a cone shape approximately 6cm long for the body. Mark the division of the legs at the front and back (without cutting through) using a no. 4 tool.

2. For the feet, divide 6g of the brown marzipan in half and roll each piece into a cone shape. Push the feet onto the legs and mark the paws with tool no. 4. Stand the body upright and push a piece of dry spaghetti down through the neck, leaving 3cm showing at the top.

3. Roll 8g of the brown marzipan into a sausage shape for the arms and cut diagonally in the centre. Turn the rounded ends under for the hands. Attach the top of the arm to the body, leaving the hands free.

4. For the coat and hat, colour 30g of marzipan with Bluebell Paste Food Colour to a dark shade of blue. Roll out the paste and cut out the coat using the template (page 48). Place this centrally over the spaghetti at the neck, keeping the straight edges to the back and front of the body. Tuck the paste neatly around the arms using the no. 4 tool, then press the paws to the body. Make a buckle from a tiny piece of marzipan tinted with Daffodil Paste Food Colour, as shown. Add some stripes on each arm and buttons down the front of the jacket.

5. For the head, roll 14g of the brown marzipan into a cone shape and ease out the cheeks, making a triangular shape. Mark the whiskers

This hound's uniform really shows off his personality. He is characterised by his cone-shaped body, triangular head, floppy ears and big tongue.

with the no. 4 tool. Divide 4g of paste in half and roll half into an oval shape for the snout. Glue in the centre of the face and mark the centre with tool no. 4. Add a small black ball for the nose and make the nostrils with tool no. 5. Roll the remaining marzipan into a cone shape and flatten with your finger. Make a straight cut at the narrow end and secure under the base of the head for the bottom lip. Push the head over the spaghetti at the neck.

6. Colour a small piece of marzipan with Poinsettia Paste Food Colour for the tongue. Roll into a small sausage shape and place inside the mouth. Mark down the centre with tool no. 4. Add a few teeth either side using white coloured marzipan. Roll two small balls of white for the eyes and place just above the nose. Paint in the pupils with Blackberry Liquid Food Colour using a fine paintbrush.

7. For the ears you will need to add some Bulrush Paste Food Colour to some of the brown marzipan you have left over. Divide 8g in half and roll each piece into a tapered cone shape. Flatten between your finger and thumb and place on either side of the head, spreading out the paste at the base.

8. Make the tail from a little Teddy Bear Brown coloured marzipan rolled into a sausage shape. Roll a little of the darker brown marzipan used for the ears onto the tip and mark with the no. 4 tool.

9. The hat is made from 4g of the dark blue marzipan. Cut out a small circle and roll a cone shape for the top. Using a little Daffodil coloured marzipan, cut out a star shape with a small cutter and glue to the hat. Secure the hat to the head.

Santa's Helpers

Materials

215g SK Marzipan

SK Dust Food Colour: Edelweiss

SK Paste Food Colours: Blackberry, Chestnut, Edelweiss, Mint, Poinsettia, Teddy Bear Brown

SK Edible Glue

Dry spaghetti

Equipment

Non-stick board and rolling pin

SK Marzipan Knife

SK Marzipan Tool Set

Paintbrush

Pizza cutter/cutting wheel

Small scissors

Foam pieces

Method

1. To make the sleigh, colour 60g of marzipan with Poinsettia Paste Food Colour, then roll out to a thickness of 0.5cm. Cut out the sleigh shape using the template (page 48). Roll out a sausage shape of red marzipan to the same width of the sleigh, lift up the front and place the sausage shape underneath. Support with a piece of foam and leave to dry. Add two round pieces on either side just above the sausage shape, as shown.

2. Colour 25g of marzipan white using Edelweiss Paste and Dust Food Colour. You will also need 25g each of Chestnut, Teddy Bear Brown, and natural (uncoloured) marzipan for the four puppies. Start by rolling 10g of your chosen colour into a cone shape for the body, then push a piece of dry spaghetti into the neck, leaving some showing to support the head.

3. Roll two small cone shapes for the back legs and add a small ball for each of the paws. Mark the paws with tool no. 4. Roll a thin sausage shape of marzipan for the front legs and turn up at each end. Cut in half and press onto the body at the front, marking the paws. Add a small tail at the back.

4. Roll 6g of marzipan into a cone shape for the head and shape with your fingers, as shown. Push over the spaghetti. To make a face with contrasting fur, place a thin teardrop shape of a different coloured marzipan over the front of the head, narrow the paste between the eyes, and mark as fur around the edges using a no. 4 tool. Mark the centre of the face with the same tool and mark the mouth on either side of the line with the curved no. 11 tool. Using tool no. 5, pull the mouth down slightly. Some of the puppies have a small oval tongue: colour a tiny

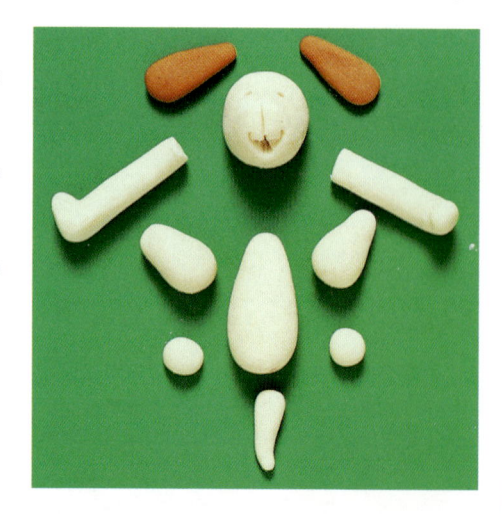

piece of marzipan pink and glue in place. Make sockets for the eyes using the no. 5 tool. Add two small black balls for the eyes and a round black nose. Make two small cone shapes for the ears and secure to the side of the head.

5. To make the large dog, colour 50g of marzipan Teddy Bear Brown. Take off 35g for the body and model it in one piece. Model the head as before and add patches in contrasting colours. Place the dog in front of the sleigh.

6. Make the harness from a thin strip of Mint coloured marzipan. Glue in place. Roll two red rails and secure to the sleigh. Wrap a green loop around the rail and secure to the dog. Dust with icing sugar to finish.

These festive dogs would make a great treat for a dog lover at Christmas time. You can, of course, change the colours of the dog and puppies to make them more like your own.

Sheepdog Chef

Materials

100g SK Marzipan

SK Dust Food Colour: Edelweiss

SK Liquid Food Colour: Blackberry

SK Paste Food Colours: Blackberry, Bluebell, Edelweiss, Poinsettia, Teddy Bear Brown

SK Edible Glue

Dry spaghetti

Equipment

Non-stick board and rolling pin

SK Marzipan Knife

SK Marzipan Tool Set

SK Sugar Dough Press

Paintbrushes

Foam pieces

Method

1. Make a small wooden spoon from 4g of marzipan coloured with Teddy Bear Brown Paste Food Colour. Roll the paste into a thin teardrop shape, then press the balled end of tool no. 3 into the widest end. Continue to thin the handle until you are happy with the shape. Set aside to dry.

2. Colour 80g of marzipan with Edelweiss Paste and Dust Food Colour. Take off 30g for the body and roll into a cone shape. Mould the cone with your fingers to create the body shape, as shown. Note that the front is quite flat. Push a piece of dry spaghetti down through the body, leaving 3cm showing at the top. Texture the paste all over with the pointed end of a no. 4 tool to create the fur.

3. Lightly paint the body with diluted Blackberry Liquid Food Colour mixed with a little Edelweiss Dust to make a pale grey shade. Leave the feet and chest white.

4. To make the apron, colour 10g of marzipan with Bluebell Paste Food Colour to a deep blue shade. Roll out and cut a 3cm square. Cut off the top two corners diagonally. Roll out a little white marzipan and cut very thin strips. Place these in a striped pattern over the apron. Make the pocket from a small blue circle cut in half and glue on the apron. Secure to the front of the dog. Cut a thin strip of blue marzipan to go around the neck and another strip to make the ties around the waist.

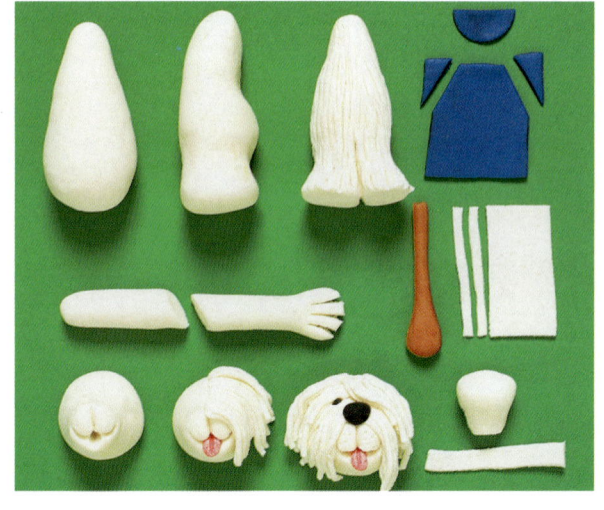

5. For the arms, roll 10g of white marzipan into a sausage shape and make a diagonal cut in the centre. Flatten both rounded ends slightly, make small cuts for the paws and round off the edges. Mark the fur on the arms with a no. 4 tool. Secure the right arm to the body and bend at the elbow. Place the wooden spoon in the left hand, wrapping the fingers and thumb around the handle. Secure the arm to the body. Support the paws with foam if necessary.

6. To make the head, roll 10g of white marzipan into a cone shape, place it on a non-stick board and flatten the front, as shown. Mark the centre with the no. 4 tool, then mark the mouth each side of the line with tool no. 11. Pull the mouth down slightly by inserting tool no. 5 inside. Make a small pink tongue and push into the hole, then mark down the centre with tool no. 5.

7. Fill a Sugar Dough press with 10g of white marzipan and extrude the strands. Brush some edible glue over the head and lay the strands of marzipan from the front of the head to the back. Continue to layer both sides and across the top. Add a black nose and make the nostrils with the no. 5 tool.

8. Make the hat from 10g of white marzipan. Take off 8g and roll into a cone shape for the top, then cut flat at the base. Make a thin band from the remainder and trim the hat. Secure to the head with edible glue.

This Old English sheepdog is similar to the 'Westie' on Top Dog, but has longer legs and more fur.

Bulldog Boss

Materials

120g SK Marzipan

SK Dust Food Colour: Edelweiss

SK Liquid Food Colour: Blackberry

SK Paste Food Colours: Blackberry, Daffodil, Edelweiss, Poinsettia, Teddy Bear Brown

SK Edible Glue

Dry spaghetti

Equipment

Non-stick board and rolling pin

SK Marzipan Knife

SK Marzipan Tool Set

Paintbrushes

Cutters: circle (small), squares (small)

Foam pieces

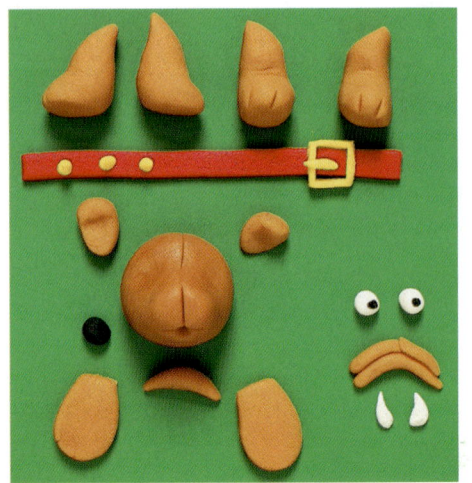

Method

1. Colour 105g of marzipan with Teddy Bear Brown Paste Food Colour. Take off 60g for the body and roll into a fat sausage shape 7cm long. Mould the body with your fingers, keeping the front thicker than the back. Pull out a tail at the back. Push a piece of spaghetti into the neck, leaving some showing to support the head.

2. For the back legs, roll 10g of the brown marzipan into a sausage shape and turn up each end for the paws. Cut in half to make the two legs. Make the front legs in exactly the same way. Support the underside of the body with a small piece of foam to lift it slightly, then attach the legs with edible glue and mark the paws with tool no. 4. The back legs should be turned out and the front legs turned slightly inwards.

3. Roll 15g of brown marzipan into a cone shape for the head and flatten at the front. To make the mouth, press a small circle cutter into the paste and pull down slightly. Using a no. 4 tool, mark the centre of the face above the mouth and continue the line to the top of the forehead.

4. Colour a small amount of marzipan white using Edelweiss Paste and Dust Food Colour. Roll two tiny white teardrop shapes for the teeth and secure each side of the mouth with edible glue.

Love or hate him, the bulldog is boss. He has a massive chest and shoulders but very short legs. Emphasise his massive eyes and wrinkled brow, not forgetting his huge jowls and teeth.

Next, add a thick bottom lip by rolling a tiny piece of brown coloured marzipan into an arch. Secure to the bottom of the mouth to exaggerate the dog's menacing look. Colour a tiny piece of marzipan black and glue in place. Mark the nostrils using tool no. 5.

5. Make two jowls by dividing 6g of brown marzipan in half. Make a teardrop shape from each piece and flatten between your fingers. Make a straight cut across the narrow end and place one either side of the line on top of the nose, bringing them down below the jaw line.

6. Make two skin folds by rolling two thin sausage shapes of marzipan. Attach these behind the nose and mark with a no. 4 tool. Roll two small balls for the eyes and place one on either side of the line above the folds. Make two teardrop shapes for eyebrows and glue over the top of the eyes. Paint the pupils with Blackberry Liquid Food Colour and a fine paintbrush.

7. For the ears, roll two teardrop shapes of brown marzipan. Keeping the rounded shape, place the ears onto the head and press a no. 1 tool inside to hollow them out. Smooth out the join at the bottom of the ear with the same tool. Push the head over the spaghetti at the neck and secure.

8. For the collar, colour a small piece of marzipan with Poinsettia Paste Food Colour and another small piece with Daffodil for the buckle and studs. Roll out the red marzipan and cut a strip 11cm long. Position the collar around the neck, overlapping the ends at the back. Make the buckle using yellow marzipan and the two smallest square cutters, as shown. Glue this to the back of the collar. Add a few studs once the collar is in place.

Kissing Kitties

Materials

130g SK Marzipan

SK Dust Food Colour: Edelweiss

SK Liquid Food Colour: Blackberry

SK Paste Food Colours: Blackberry, Bluebell, Edelweiss, Poinsettia

SK Edible Glue

Dry spaghetti

Equipment

Non-stick board and rolling pin

SK Marzipan Knife

SK Marzipan Tool Set

Paintbrushes

White floristry stamens

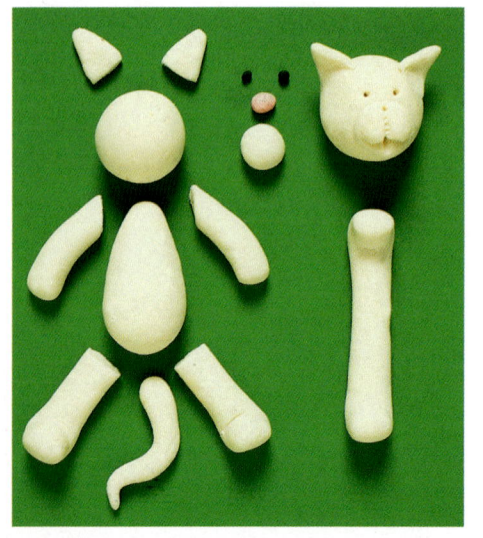

Method

1. Colour 130g of marzipan white using Edelweiss Dust and Paste Food Colour. Take off 20g for the girl kitten's body and roll into a cone shape. Stand upright and push a piece of dry spaghetti down through the body, leaving 3cm showing at the top for the head.

2. For the legs, roll 12g of white marzipan into a sausage shape, turn up the rounded ends and cut in half. Brush the ends with edible glue and push onto the body. Roll 8g into a sausage shape for the arms, cut diagonally in the centre and secure to the sides of the body.

3. To make the head, roll 14g of the white marzipan into a ball. Slip this over the spaghetti at the neck. Roll another small ball and place this in the centre of the face. Using tool no. 12, mark the centre of this ball, then press the smaller end of tool no. 11 gently on either side of the line for the mouth. Insert tool no. 5 in-between and pull down slightly to make a hole for the tongue. Colour 4g of white marzipan with a little Poinsettia Paste Food Colour, take off a tiny amount and make a small oval shape for the tongue. Push into the mouth and mark with tool no. 4.

4. To make the ears, roll two small teardrop shapes of white, flatten with your finger, make a straight cut at the widest end and secure to the head. Indent with tool no. 1 and smooth the join. Add a small ball of pink for the nose and make the nostrils with the end of tool no. 5. Make two holes for the eyes using tool no. 5 and fill with tiny balls of black marzipan.

5. For the tail, roll 4g of white marzipan into a tapered sausage shape and secure to the back of the kitten. Cut four white flower stamens in

half and insert them into the face for whiskers. Add the pads to the base of each paw by rolling tiny balls of marzipan and pressing them in place.

6. Make the boy kitten in exactly the same way and entwine his tail with hers. The right arm of the boy kitten should be secured to the back of the girl kitten.

7. Dilute some Blackberry Liquid Food Colour with water and paint on the stripes with a fine paintbrush. Paint the tip of the kittens' tails in blue or pink and add a touch of colour inside the ears.

These cute kittens are made from white marzipan and their markings painted on afterwards. If you're celebrating an engagement, this couple makes a great cake top decoration or keepsake.

Purrrfectly Matched

Materials

280g SK Marzipan

SK Dust Food Colours: Edelweiss, Silver (Metallic Lustre)

SK Liquid Food Colours: Blackberry, Bulrush, Poinsettia

SK Paste Food Colours: Blackberry, Bluebell, Edelweiss, Mint, Poinsettia, Sunflower, Teddy Bear Brown

SK Edible Glue

Dry spaghetti

Equipment

Non-stick board and rolling pin

SK Marzipan Knife

SK Marzipan Tool Set

SK Sugar Dough Press

Paintbrushes

Cutters: blossom, circle (small), leaf (large)

Textured rolling pin (optional)

Floristry stamens: black and white

24 gauge floristry wire

Method

1. Colour 200g of marzipan with Blackberry Paste Food Colour and 70g with Edelweiss Dust and Paste Food Colour. This will be enough for both cats.

2. To make the groom's body, roll 60g of black marzipan into a cone 6cm long. Push a length of dry spaghetti down through the body, leaving 3cm showing at the neck. Make the feet from 8g of white marzipan and mark the paws with a no. 4 tool. For the chest area, thinly roll out 4g of white marzipan and cut out a large leaf shape. Place on the front of the body and smooth the edges.

3. For the arms, roll 10g of black marzipan into a sausage shape and cut diagonally in the centre. Make two hands from 6g of white marzipan. Using tool no. 4, cut a thumb and three fingers,

continued on page 38

These newlyweds would look splendid atop a wedding or anniversary cake. You can, of course, change the colour of the cats if desired.

round off the edges and push a small piece of dry spaghetti into each wrist. Secure the paws to the arms with edible glue. Bend the left arm out and place the hand on the hip. The right hand should have the fingers positioned so that the cane can be held between the thumb and finger. Support with foam if necessary until dry.

4. Roll the head from 18g of black marzipan and mark the centre of the face below the nose area with tool no. 4. Make two cone shapes from 4g of white, flatten slightly and secure either side of the line. Add a bottom lip, as shown. Push tool no. 5 into the mouth area to make a small hole for the tongue. Roll a tiny pink cone shape and push into the hole, then mark with tool no. 4. Add a pink button for the nose and make the nostrils with tool no. 5. Roll two small oval shapes for the eyes and add a black pupil in each. Paint the detail on the mouth and cheeks using a little diluted Teddy Bear Brown Paste Food Colour. Cut some white stamens in half for whiskers and push into the cheeks.

5. Make the cane and tail from 6g of black divided equally. For the cane, roll a tapered sausage shape of black marzipan and push a piece of dry spaghetti through the middle for support. Secure a white knob on the end and allow to dry. Roll a tapered sausage for the tail and glue a white tip on the end. Attach to the back of the body. When the cane is dry, place inside the hand.

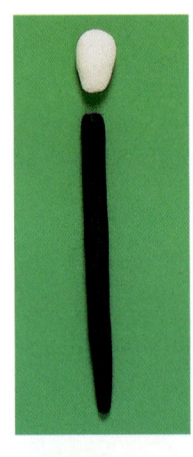

6. For the hat, roll out 4g of black marzipan and cut out a brim using a small circle cutter. Roll a thick sausage for the main part of the hat and cut to size. Cut a thin strip for the band and secure to the hat. Glue in place and brush with Silver Lustre Dust using a dry paintbrush.

7. Colour 4g of marzipan with Poinsettia Paste Food Colour for the bow tie. Roll out and cut a strip measuring 1cm x 5cm, fold both ends into the centre, turn over and pinch the middle with your finger and thumb. Mark the creases with a no. 4 tool, as shown. Secure in place with edible glue.

8. To make the bride, follow the same basic instructions as for the groom, but divide the body at the base to make two short legs. Round off the ends with your fingers, then add the paws. The facial features for the bride are slightly different: make the nose rounded, colour the eyes blue, add small pink eyelids over the eyes and paint on eyelashes with a fine brush and Bulrush Liquid Food Colour. Add black stamens for the whiskers.

9. Colour 4g of marzipan with Mint Paste Food Colour, place inside a Sugar Dough press and extrude long pieces for flower stalks. Arrange the stalks under and over the left arm and glue in place. For the flowers, roll out 4g of pink coloured marzipan and cut out three flowers using a small blossom cutter. Mark each petal with a no. 5 tool and add a small dot of yellow in the centre. Secure in place.

10. For the veil, roll out 10g of white marzipan and cut out a 5cm square piece. If required, give the veil a pattern using a textured rolling pin. Gather the marzipan at the top and secure to the head. Add a pink bow. Roll tiny balls of yellow marzipan and push them together to make a necklace.

Projects

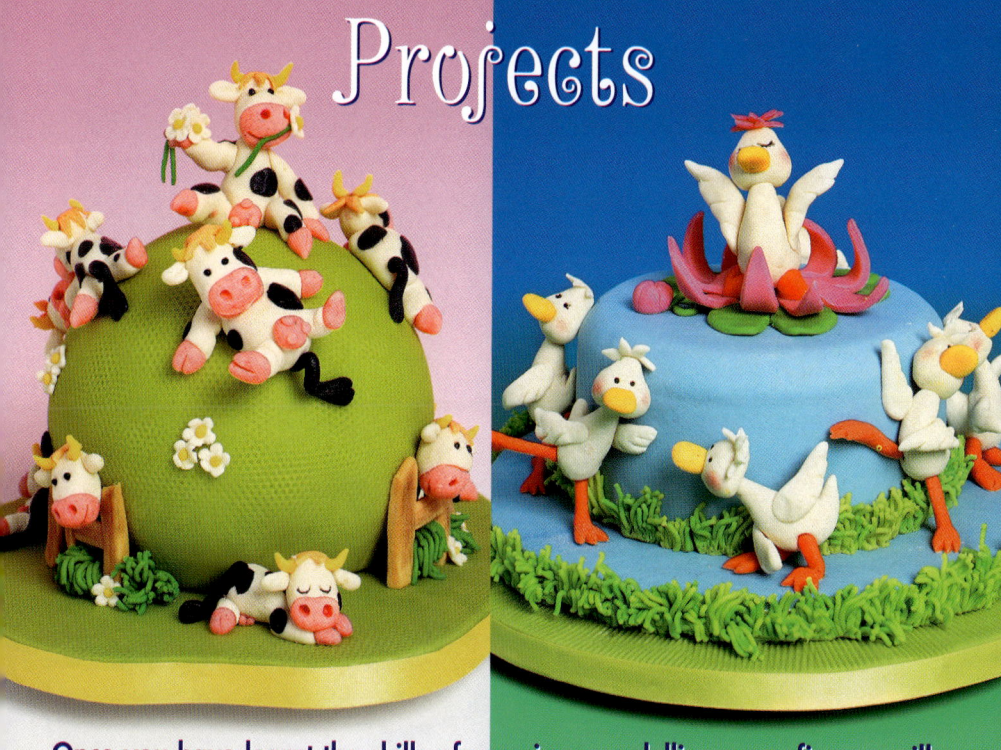

Once you have learnt the skills of marzipan modelling, your figures will look great on a cake! Here, I have made four cakes with some of the animals shown earlier in the book. I have chosen the themes spring, summer, autumn and winter, but you can create your own theme and use the models on your own individual designs.

Moo Cow Meadow

Materials

2 x 1 litre basin cakes

1.1kg SK Marzipan

SK Dust Food Colour: Edelweiss

SK Paste Food Colours: Black, Edelweiss, Fuchsia, Leaf Green, Mint, Sunflower, Teddy Bear Brown

Equipment

25cm petal shaped cake drum

Non-stick board and rolling pin

SK Marzipan Knife

SK Marzipan Tool Set

SK Sugar Dough Press

SK Texture Boards

Pizza cutter/cutting wheel

Blossom cutter

Small calyx cutter

Small circle cutter

15mm yellow ribbon

Method

1. Colour 650g of marzipan with Leaf Green Paste Food Colour. Take off 300g for the drum and set the rest aside. Cover the cake drum (see page 6), then press one of the texture boards into the paste around the edges to make a pattern. Trim the edges with a marzipan knife. Roll out the remaining green marzipan and cover the cake. Trim neatly around the base, taking care to smooth out any pleats. Roll the covered cake between the texture boards to create a pattern on the surface.

2. To make the fences, you will need to colour 120g of marzipan with a little Teddy Bear Brown Paste Food Colour. Roll out to an even 0.5cm thickness, then cut into 5cm x 1cm strips using a pizza cutter or cutting wheel. Mark with tool no. 4 to resemble wood. Make three fences and position them evenly around the base of the cake. To make the grass, colour 12g of marzipan with Mint Paste Food Colour. Extrude the marzipan through a Sugar Dough press, cut off short pieces and arrange under the fence. Secure with edible glue.

3. Colour 265g of marzipan white using both Edelweiss Paste and Dust Food Colour. Mix thoroughly. This will be enough for eleven cows and the daisies. Make the cows (see pages 14-15) and arrange in different positions around the cake and board. Where there is a fence, only the head and tail are visible (there is no need to make the whole cow).

4. Finally, make a few daisies using the blossom cutter. Place around the cake and secure with edible glue. Trim the board with yellow ribbon.

Spring

Ducks on Swan Lake

Materials

15cm round cake

1.63kg SK Marzipan

SK Dust Food Colours: Edelweiss, Pastel Pink, Rose

SK Liquid Food Colour: Blackberry

SK Paste Food Colours: Blackberry, Bluebell, Edelweiss, Leaf Green, Nasturtium, Rose, Sunflower, Vine

SK Edible Glue

Dry spaghetti

Equipment

25.5cm and 30.5cm round cake drums

Non-stick board and rolling pin

Ribbed rolling pin (optional)

SK Marzipan Knife

SK Marzipan Tool Set

SK Sugar Dough Press

Calyx cutter

Small cake card

Foam pieces

15mm width green ribbon

Method

1. Colour 800g of marzipan with Bluebell Paste Food Colour. Cover the smaller cake drum and the cake with the blue marzipan and place the cake in the centre of the board.

2. For the larger cake drum, colour 300g of marzipan with Leaf Green Paste Food Colour. Roll the marzipan into a strip long enough to go all around the edge of the board and place in position. Overlap the ends and make a clean cut through both ends with a marzipan knife. Using a ribbed rolling pin, texture the strip (this is optional). Place the cake and smaller board centrally on the larger board.

3. Colour 200g of marzipan with Vine Paste Food Colour for the grass. Fill a Sugar Dough press with the green marzipan and squeeze out short strands. Cut off and glue around the base of the cake and the edge of the smaller board.

4. Colour 250g of marzipan white using both Edelweiss Dust and Paste Food Colour, 40g Nasturtium, 10g Sunflower and 4g Blackberry. This will be enough to make all the ducks. Make the ducks in different positions for the sides of the cake (see pages 16-17). The duck on the top is slightly larger and has pink calyx shapes for the feathers.

5. Roll out some green coloured marzipan and cut out three lily pads using the template (page 48).

Mark with tool no. 4 and place onto a small cake card. For the water lily, colour 25g of marzipan with Rose Paste Food Colour and roll out quite thinly. Cut out the petals using the template (page 48) and place over a rolling pin to dry in a curved shape. When dry, attach the petals to the centre of the lily pad with edible glue and support with foam if necessary.

6. Glue the lily pads and water lily on top of the cake. Place the larger duck in the centre and the other ducks around the sides of the cake. Trim the board with green ribbon.

Summer

Hibernating Happy Hedgehogs

Materials

Cake baked in 15cm diameter terracotta plant pot

1.12kg SK Marzipan

SK Dust Food Colours: Bulrush, Chestnut, Rose, Soft Peach

SK Liquid Food Colour: Bulrush

SK Paste Food Colours: Blackberry, Daffodil, Holly/Ivy, Terracotta

SK Edible Glue

Equipment

23cm round cake drum

Non-stick board and rolling pin

SK Marzipan Knife

SK Marzipan Tool Set

2.5cm circle cutter

Tweezers

Veiner (optional)

Tin foil

15mm width gold ribbon

Method

1. Colour 250g of marzipan with Holly/Ivy Paste Food Colour, roll out and cover the cake drum. Level the top of the cake, then turn it upside down. Colour 550g of marzipan with Terracotta Paste Food Colour and use 400g (14oz) to cover the cake. Roll out the remaining paste and cut a strip measuring 46cm x 4cm. Wrap the strip around the base of the pot and neaten the join at the back. Secure the cake to the centre of the board.

2. Using a 2.5cm round cutter, cut out a circle in the top of the plant pot. This is where the hedgehog will climb out. Using a soft, dry brush, dust the board with Bulrush Dust Food Colour to resemble soil.

3. To make the leaves, thinly roll out 130g of Holly/Ivy coloured marzipan. Using the templates (page 48), cut out five each of A and B and fifteen of C. Make veins in the leaves with a veiner or tool no. 4. Scrunch up some foil and lay the leaves on top to dry. When dry, dust with Chestnut and Bulrush Dust Food Colours.

4. Colour 40g of marzipan with Bulrush Paste Food Colour to make five acorns. Take a small piece and roll it into an oval, then roll a smaller piece into a ball to make the acorn cup. Using tool no. 3, hollow out the cup and place the acorn inside. Using a pair of tweezers, pinch all over the cup to make it spiky.

5. Make a hedgehog (see pages 22-23) to sit on the board, then follow the same method to make a smaller hedgehog (use approximately 55g of marzipan). Secure the hedgehogs in place with edible glue.

6. Arrange the leaves and acorns around the cake and secure with edible glue. Trim the board with gold ribbon.

Autumn

45

Sleigh Ride

Materials

15cm x 20.5cm oval cake

1.1kg SK Marzipan

SK Paste Food Colours: Blackberry, Mint, Poinsettia, Teddy Bear Brown, Yucca

SK Edible Glue

Equipment

25.5cm x 30.5cm oval board

Non-stick board and rolling pin

SK Marzipan Knife

SK Marzipan Tool Set

Pizza cutter/cutting wheel

2cm holly leaf cutter

Fine scissors

Cocktail stick

15mm width red ribbon

Method

1. Colour 800g of marzipan white using both Edelweiss Paste and Dust Food Colour. Cover the board and cake, then secure the cake to the board.

2. Make the holly leaves to cover the cake and board using leftover white marzipan. Roll out thinly and cut out the leaves using a holly cutter. Arrange the leaves in threes around the cake and board and secure in place with edible glue. Mark the leaves with tool no. 4. Colour 30g of marzipan with Poinsettia Paste Food Colour to make the berries. Roll three small balls for each cluster and glue in the centre of the leaves.

3. Make the sleigh, puppies and dog (see pages 28-29) and place on top of the cake.

4. To make the trees, colour 55g of marzipan with Yucca Paste Food Colour. Divide the paste, making one piece slightly larger than the other. Take one piece, make a cone shape, then insert a cocktail stick into the base. Starting at the top of the tree, cut into the paste at 45° using fine scissors. Continue all the way around, then work down the cone until complete. Remove the cocktail stick and secure the tree to the cake. Make a second tree using the same technique.

5. Finish the cake with a light dusting of icing sugar. Trim the board with red ribbon.

Winter

Sleigh Ride
Sleigh

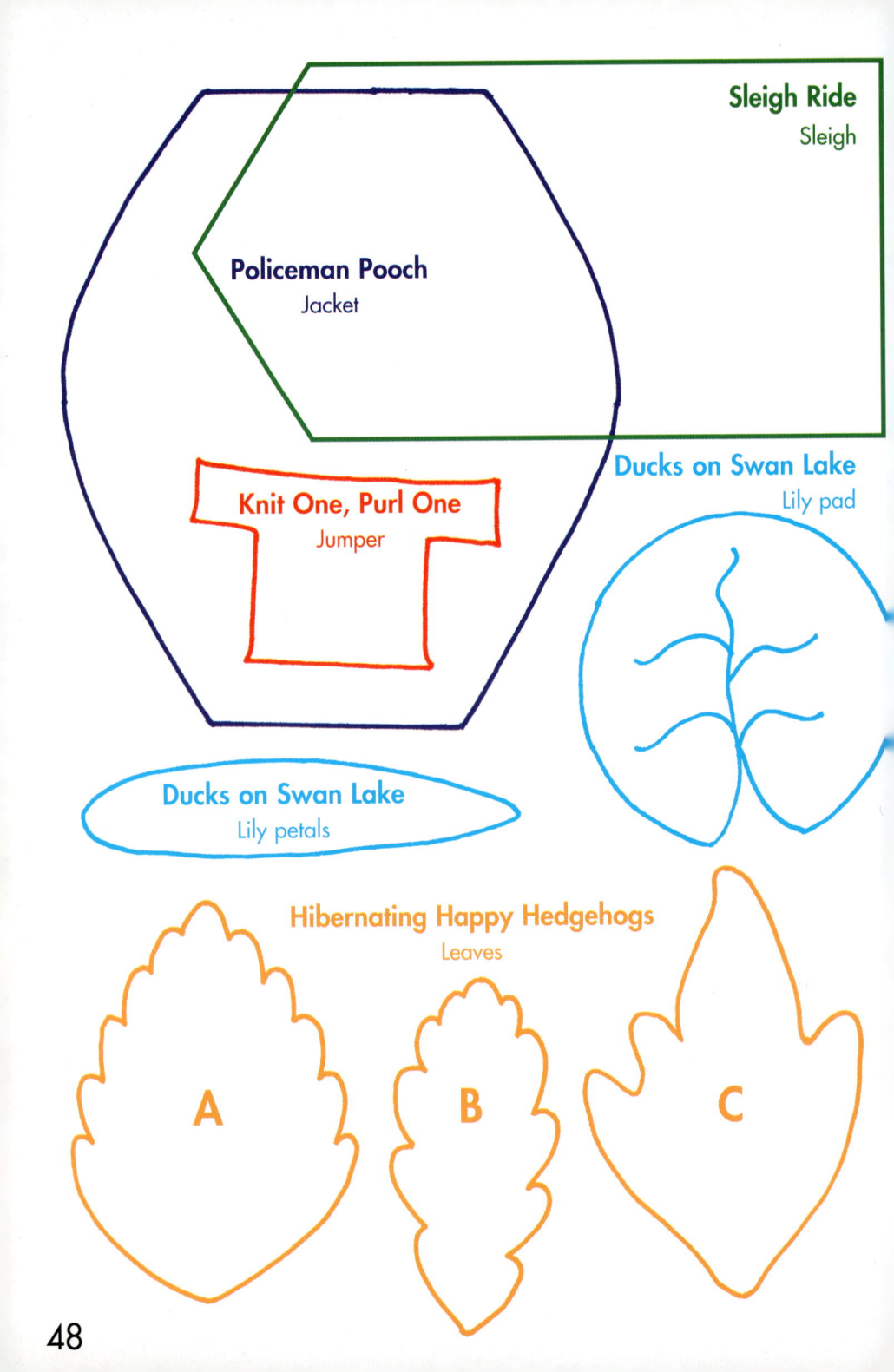

Policeman Pooch
Jacket

Knit One, Purl One
Jumper

Ducks on Swan Lake
Lily pad

Ducks on Swan Lake
Lily petals

Hibernating Happy Hedgehogs
Leaves

A B C

48